dedicated to

all the people—

young and old—*who have a*

Passion
FOR THE
Game

HONOR
BOOKS

Passion for the Game

ISBN 1-56292-848-1
Copyright © 2000 VisionQuest Communications Group, Inc.
and Koechel Peterson & Associates

Published by Honor Books
P.O. Box 55388
Tulsa, Oklahoma 74155

Research, Information, and Transcriptions:
Mary Ann Van Meter, LeAnn Fisher, Jennifer Lewellen,
and Annette Glavan

Text Editing: Lance Wubbels and John Humphrey

All quotes from current players are taken from interviews
conducted for various VisionQuest programs and projects.

Cover and interior design by Koechel Peterson & Associates
Minneapolis, Minnesota.

Little League photos on pages 8-9 courtesy of Darvin Edwards.

When written in Chinese, the word "crisis" is composed of two characters: One represents danger; the other represents opportunity.

So it is for those who have the heart of a champion and a passion for the game.

A champion is one who looks at a situation and sees a challenge when those around him see a problem. It's all a matter of perspective.

That's what *Passion for the Game* is all about—athletes using their platform to have a positive influence on others. This book is not about statistics and salaries; it's about the people who play baseball because they have a passion for the game. It's about those who also want to let their lives be virtuous examples. It's about what's good about baseball. It's about character.

The men you'll hear from here epitomize this. I played with and against many of them during my big league career. I've had the opportunity to get to know others through my work in television.

Each of the men on these pages gives us something to feel good about in sports. This book grabs the images and memories of yesterday and today, and holds them until tomorrow. As well, the men who make the memories, themselves, share truths that are timeless. For a moment, time stands still, side by side with truths that stand eternal.

I hope after reading this book, you, too, will develop a new, or renewed, passion for the game of baseball. I also hope the insight and truth shared by my friends will have an impact on your life that will go beyond nine innings.

HAROLD REYNOLDS
Baseball Analyst, ESPN

Leading Off

Time is of the essence. The shadow moves

From the plate to the box, from the box to second base,

From second to the outfield, to the bleachers.

Time is of the essence. The crowd and players

Are the same age always, but the man in the crowd

Is older every season. Come on, play ball!

From "Polo Grounds" by Rolfe Humphries

Baseball is a president tossing out the first ball of the season, and a scrubby schoolboy playing catch with his dad on a Mississippi farm. A tall, thin old man waving a scorecard from the corner of his dugout—that's baseball. So is a big fat guy with a bulbous nose running home one of his 714 home runs.

There's a man in Mobile who remembers that Honus Wagner hit a triple in Pittsburgh forty-six years ago—that's baseball. And so is the scout reporting that a sixteen-year-old sandlot pitcher in Cheyenne is the coming Walter Johnson.

Baseball is a spirited race of man against man, reflex against reflex—a game of inches. Every skill is measured. Every heroic, every failing, is seen and cheered or booed, and then becomes a statistic.

In baseball, democracy shines its clearest. The only race that matters is the race to the bag. The creed is a rule book and color merely something to distinguish one team's uniform from another.

Baseball is a rookie (his experience no bigger than the lump in his throat) as he begins fulfillment of his dream. It's a veteran, too—a tired old man of thirty-five hoping those aching muscles can pull him through another sweltering August and September.

Nicknames are baseball: names like Zeek and Pie and Kiki, and Home Run and Cracker and Dizzy and Dazzy.

Baseball is the clear cool eyes of Rogers Hornsby, the flashing spikes of Ty Cobb, and an over-age pixie named Rabbit Maranville.

Baseball—just a game as simple as a ball and bat, and yet as complex as the American spirit it symbolizes. It's a sport, a business, and sometimes almost even a religion.

The fairy tale of Willie Mays making a brilliant World Series catch and then dashing off to play stickball in the streets with his teenage pals—that's baseball. So is the husky voice of a doomed Lou Gehrig saying, "I consider myself the luckiest man on the face of this earth."

Baseball is cigar smoke, hot-roasted peanuts, *The Sporting News*, Ladies Day, Down in Front, "Take Me Out to the Ball Game," and "The Star Spangled Banner."

Baseball is a man named Campanella telling the nation's business leaders, "You have to be a man to be a big leaguer, but you have to have a lot of little boy in you, too." This is a game for America, this baseball—a game for boys and for men.

ERNIE HARWELL
Hall of Fame broadcaster for the Detroit Tigers

First INNING

What is it about baseball that makes this game such an integral and special part of American life?

Baseball is a game for the ages. It is unchanging from generation to generation. It is a part of the American fabric, now woven into that of other cultures as well. From the moment a boy picks up a bat or a ball, something about this sport grips him.

Baseball ties the past to the present, to the future; and ties us to both, and to each other.

"Well——it's our game; that's the chief fact in connection with it;

America's game; it has the snap, go, fling of the American atmosphere;

it belongs as much to our institutions, fits into them as significantly as our

Constitution's laws; is just as important in the sum total of our historic life."

WALT WHITMAN

Today, fathers still teach baseball to their children the same way their fathers once taught them. The game is handed down from within a family as a valuable heirloom. In a time in which change happens in the blink of an eye all around us, baseball, the unchanging game, brings families together like no other sport or game can.

No other sport initiates such devotion to statistics and trivia. Where else will man, woman, or child spend so many hours poring over box scores day after day? Where else will a child peer through a backstop three hours before a game, watching grown men prepare to play a child's game? Where else do women deftly wield pencil and eraser to track every pitch, keeping score in a dog-eared program? Where else do presidents throw out the first ball? For what other sport have historians, novelists, poets, and essayists— or for that matter, butchers, bakers, and candlestick makers—attempted to explain our love for such a game?

"In the major leagues, there are only going to be

eight hundred players of the best from the world.

If you want to be in that class, you have to work hard."

SANDY ALOMAR JR.

On sandlots in cities across America, set against the back-drop of dusk-filled skies, boys and girls give endless hours to the game with nothing more than a bat and a ball. In streets throughout the Bronx, a sawed-off broomstick is all that's needed. In the fields of America's heartland, a diminutive fielder battles the cornstalk outfield to make a catch. In the backyards of California, a father and son play catch before dinner. In the Dominican Republic, future Sammy Sosas take turn hitting a pitched bundle of socks with a tree branch, while a fielder scurries across land once inhabited by sugar cane and adjusts the flattened milk carton that serves as a makeshift glove. In St. Louis, 45,000 devoted fans—young and old alike—rise in unison as Mark McGwire steps up to the plate. Around America, and beyond its borders, baseball is joined by one common thread from all who watch or play—a passion for the game.

Baseball is poetry and symmetry. It incorporates ballet-like movement with power, speed, pinpoint accuracy, hustle, and perseverance.

"My mama's got a picture of me in Pampers, holding a bat."

RANDY VELARDE

Like a classic literary work or film, it is filled with drama and suspense, strategy and mystery, antagonists and heroes, failure and redemption. The game itself, and the history within, are timeless, and create timeless discussions, timeless passion.

We are captivated by questions we cannot answer, debates that last decades, speculations we will take to our graves. Who is better—Mays or Griffey? Maddux or Koufax? '61 Yankees or '98 Yankees?

Baseball is numbers. 162 games, 9 innings, 3 outs, 3 strikes, 4 balls. 714, .403, 1947, 40/40, 2,131, 4,192, 70…

Baseball is a game of love. A game of passion.

The galleries of our minds capture and hold forever the heroes of our youth, the memories of childhood. No other game does this like baseball.

Second
INNING

The passion for this game is fueled
by the wonder of the game itself.

"I remember [when I was] four or five
years old, when my dad brought me
down to Crosely Field. I mean, I looked
up to those guys. Those guys were
superhuman to me. And now I realize
that some of these kids look up at
us in the same way."
PAUL O'NEILL

"When I was a boy growing up in
Kansas, a friend of mine and I went
fishing, and as we sat there in the
warmth of a summer afternoon we
talked about what we wanted to do
when we grew up. I told him I wanted
to be a real major league baseball
player, a genuine professional like
Honus Wagner. My friend said he'd
like to be president of the United
States. Neither of us got our wish."
DWIGHT D. EISENHOWER

Baseball is first embraced when we are young. It is a game we grow up with. Before we can shoot a basket, catch a touchdown pass, or sink a putt, we have learned how to throw a ball and swing a bat. Forever after, we think of baseball as part of the happiest and most carefree days of our lives.

Perhaps there is no norm for players of such a demanding game. Yet for each of the thousands who've ever seen their name emblazoned across the back of a big league uniform jersey, it all began with a dream.

From the first time the ball is held, the first game ever played, the dream takes hold. For every young boy or girl who ever scampered around the bases and felt what it was like to touch home plate and be mobbed by teammates; for everyone who streaked across the outfield grass, thrust an arm out, opened their eyes and saw the ball was indeed in the glove; for every wide-eyed youngster who ever held an autographed hat or glove or ball; for every Little Leaguer, high schooler, or college player—the dream has gripped them. It is the dream that one day they, too, might play this child's game as their vocation.

It seizes us. Jim Bouton perhaps said it best: "You spend a good piece of your life gripping a baseball, and it turns out it was the other way around all the time." The hold that baseball has on us is almost mesmerizing, yet it is simply the passion for the game working its magic.

"That was my dream, being able to wear the uniform of a professional team. But to get to the major leagues and play as long as I have is beyond what I thought."

TONY FERNANDEZ

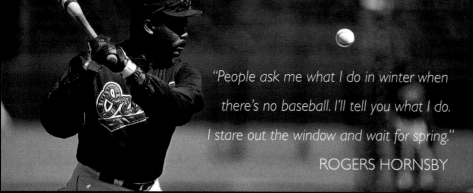

Third INNING

It is an afternoon in mid-March. The sky is clear and a brilliant blue. The sun's warm slanting rays begin to lift the slight chill of winter's hangover. The sweet smell of fresh-cut grass saturates the air. A steadily growing crowd entering and finding seats in the old grandstand provides a constant hum like a swarm of bees. The anticipation of a new beginning is thick. Covered in shadows, with the sunlit field before them, fans gaze upon the thick, well-manicured green—even the old diamond looks new. No wind stirs the long leaves of the palm trees beyond the chain-link fence that encases the outfield.

"The most exciting moment in my career was when they told me I was being promoted to the major leagues."

VLADIMIR GUERRERO

"I was a 45th-round draft pick, who for most of the time they didn't really look at. But then I had the opportunity to show I had some tools."

CHAD CURTIS

"If you'd asked me if I was going to be in professional baseball thirty plus years, it would have been hard to believe. To be blessed and fortunate enough to be in this game to start with, and then to last this long, it's really satisfying. I've been fortunate enough to put on this uniform and walk into major league clubhouses that a lot of men, women, and children alike would die to be able to do."

JOHNNY OATES

In the fourth row of the grandstand on the first-base side of home plate, the faithful rest in seats more comfortable to the soul than the body. Thin cast-iron arms frame hard plastic pull-down seats. Yet none of the discomfort matters. It is spring, and all is well in the world for baseball fans. Dreams of pennant chases are renewed. So is the career of a slightly over-the-hill pitcher trying to coax one last season out of his arm. Minor league phenoms bask in the amber glare of a new audience to impress. It is ultimate baseball bliss. A 6-15 pitching record, a .213 batting average, and a 58-104 season finish are distant memories. Every team and player starts afresh. As hope springs eternal, so it is that spring brings eternal hope. This will be the year.

It has been estimated that one out of every five hundred Little Leaguers ever makes it to the major leagues. This is the place where the select few see their dreams realized. But it can be short-lived. The average major league career is less than two years. For every Tony Gwynn or Cal Ripken there is Joe Charboneau or Clint Hartung. Yet each is driven by a passion for the game and the chance that he just might one day make it to "the show."

"I think everybody at one time or another has been considered a prospect. Obviously, you're not up here just by accident. And how you handle that personally has a lot to do with how you're going to do."
RANDY VELARDE

"This is where you want to be. You get treated a lot better; the travel is a lot better; the money is obviously a lot better. It's your ultimate goal. The minors are so bad that you want to get out, and it gives you motivation to get better at this game."
TODD WALKER

"I was sleeping in the hotel during my time in Double A, and they knocked on my door at 1 A.M. and told me that I had been called to the big team. That night I couldn't sleep anymore."
ABRAHAM NUNEZ

Fourth INNING

A passion for this game has burned ever since the days a few thousand derby-hatted men in rickety wooden grandstands watched young men named Matthewson, Cobb, Wagner, and Ruth. It burned as this game grew into a burgeoning industry, played out in ornate temples before millions from all races, ages, nationalities, and genders. It burns now as impressive athletic specimens named Sosa, McGwire, Griffey, Martinez, and Jeter take away our breath.

"I never wanted to fall short for the fans' sake. The one thing I want to be remembered [for] most of all is that Gary Carter gave it his all."
GARY CARTER

Fans. Their abiding loyalty to the pastime is shown in their persistent, sometimes comical, attachment to the sport. The word "fan" itself has a sort of colloquial affability. None of us can quite identify with the noisy, cheerful, or irritable mob at the park, which includes children, front-runners, critics, and experts. Among them, though, are the fans—those whose attention and memory give each game its resonance.

Baseball is a family for those who follow it. Neither race, age, nor gender is delineated within this family. Like a melting pot, the stadium brings them together—fathers and sons, brothers and sisters, grandparents and wide-eyed toddlers. It can be seen in their eyes, through their expressions. All share the bond of a passion for the game.

"The enjoyment I get from the camaraderie with the fans—everywhere I go, people wish me well. 'I'm pulling for you. I'm glad you beat this [cancer]. I'll continue to pray for you.' No matter where I am—home or away—it's all genuine. To interact with those fans, that's the best thing."
ERIC DAVIS

Baseball is like a living museum—a collection of moments etched in time and in the recesses of our souls. It's three stunning Reggie Jackson home runs in October. It's the flash of a Nolan Ryan fastball. It's Bill Buckner looking despondently between his legs for the one that got away. It's Jackie Robinson smiling through the taunts; Jimmy Piersall running around the bases backward; "The Giants Win the Pennant!"; the amazing Mets, and Cal Ripken's game 2131. Baseball is Sammy Sosa and Mark McGwire bringing two cultures together through homers and hugs. It is ordinary men, achieving extraordinary feats and creating indelible memories.

"I think the biggest support, the greatest support, has to be the fans. The fans would write me in the moments I was down. They helped me a lot."

TONY OLIVA

"I care about the fans, about the people, because those people that you see up there (in the stands), those people pay our salary. They give me a lot of motivation in right field. Sometimes when I'm 0 for 4, 0 for 5, I hear somebody say, 'Don't worry about it—you are the man!' That right there motivates me."

SAMMY SOSA

HOW TO IDENTITY A REAL FAN

1. Has a passion for the game.
2. Plans spring vacations around the Houston Astros spring training schedule.
3. Goes to the ballpark early to watch the team's infield practice.
4. Favorite T-shirt says "Property of Chicago Cubs."
5. Has enjoyed a ten-year subscription to The Baseball Digest.
6. Has "Take Me Out to the Ballgame" programmed as the ringer on his cell phone and pager.
7. Thinks Sparky Anderson would have made a good president.
8. Would love to take a job as a stadium usher.
9. Carries his 1957 Brooks Robinson card in his wallet.
10. Knows who Andy Kosco is.
11. Still proudly displays Little League trophies.
12. Would rather visit Fenway Park than the Taj Mahal.
13. Took transistor radio to school as a kid, to secretly listen to World Series games during class.
14. Still has dreams of pitching for the Los Angeles Dodgers.
15. At ballgames, sees the look of wonder on a child's face and remembers how it felt.
16. Owns several teams in various rotisserie leagues.
17. Has a full collection of trading cards dating back to 1961.
18. Says life's greatest thrill was meeting Mickey Mantle.
19. Made bid on the internet for autographed Mark McGwire home run ball.
20. Stops to see a Little League game even though he has no children of his own.

Fifth INNING

Baseball bats have no purpose outside of the game. On their own, they are useless. They are not good for table legs, walking canes, or doorposts. Every tree that gives its life for a batch of bats has a special and singular purpose. Alone, rounded shafts of ash are simply that. But in the hands of a Williams, Musial, or Carew, they become instruments of artistry.

"Catchers are there everyday, and they come to play. They're the guys that people don't see very often, but they mean so much to the team. To me, catching is my work, it's my job... getting down and dirty, balls hitting you, and everything else."
CHARLES JOHNSON

"See the ball, hit the ball."
ERIC DAVIS

Thus begins the odyssey of perfecting the most difficult discipline in all of sports—using a round bat to hit a round ball squarely. The best hitters in the world are successful only 30 percent of the time. In any other sport, this would be considered failure. Yet, we marvel at those who make it happen. They are virtuosos; athletic prodigies who are awesome to observe, but not particularly rewarding to over-analyze. After all, one can take apart a wristwatch, but not a sunset.

A glove is but a swatch of cowhide. Yet to a fielder, it becomes a lifelong friend—one he talks to and coddles with the most delicate of care, as if trying to coax it into not letting him down. Together they go from satire to the sublime; more often than not making the spectacular look routine.

The catcher's mask, shin guards, and chest protector are collectively known as the "tools of ignorance." Yet those who don them are some of the most intelligent men in the game, who often become the best managers. After all, only the catcher sees the whole game at all times.

A ball is a five-ounce, nine-inch assimilation of scrap material—a small piece of cork wrapped in fine yarn, covered with horsehide, and stitched tightly together with red thread. Its aerodynamics, combined with pitchers' hands and an occasional assist from the wind, can make it dip, drop, curve, slide, knuckle, and generally baffle the best of hitters. But when the hitter catches up with it, look out. No facet of any sport is the subject of so much frustration and so such bliss.

"When I was a kid my dad used to tell me about Willie Mays. And Willie Mays used to say, 'If I don't beat you with my bat, I'll beat you with my glove. If I don't beat you with my glove, I'll beat you with my legs.'"
TRAVIS FRYMAN

"Challenging a hitter is part of the game. You've got to do that if you want to be a successful pitcher in the big leagues."
PEDRO MARTINEZ

These are the tools of the trade. No two players use them exactly alike. Yet as diverse as the use of these tools is, so are the men who make memories with them.

Baseball is tradition—the national anthem, throwing out the first pitch, the seventh-inning stretch. It is stepping over the baseline when running on and off the field. It's not talking to a pitcher when he has a no-hitter going through six innings.

Baseball is the game inside the game. There's the emotional struggle of battling an 0-18 slump; the chess match between managers aligning pitchers versus hitters; stepping out of the bullpen with the bases loaded and the game on the line. On this field, players are set apart.

"I've worked on the same things ever since I've been in high school— to try to consistently go up there and hit the ball hard. If I change everything and try to start aiming the ball, I'm not helping anybody, and I'm probably hurting myself. It's a game. It's repetition."

PAUL O'NEILL
1994 A.L. Batting Champion

"I try to simplify it as much as possible. The only train of thought I have is to see the ball as good as I can and hit the ball back up the middle. Usually, that works."

ALEX RODRIGUEZ
1996 A.L. Batting Champion

DID YOU KNOW THAT...

- **Babe Ruth** once led the American League in earned run average as a pitcher in 1916, going 23-13 with a 1.75 ERA.

- **Hack Wilson** is the shortest home run champ in major league history at 5'6".

- In his first game as baseball's first African American manager, Hall of Famer **Frank Robinson** inserted himself into the lineup and homered to lead his Cleveland Indians to a 5-3 defeat of the Yankees on opening day, April 7, 1975.

- **Mickey Mantle's** salary in 1956, the year he won the triple crown, was $32,500.

- **Joe Torre** is the first manager to lose 1,000 games before winning 1,000.

- **Ken Griffey Jr.** and **Stan Musial** not only hail from the same birthplace (Donora, Pennsylvania) but they also share the same birthday (November 21).

- All-Star catcher **Mike Piazza** was selected in the 62nd round of the 1988 amatuer draft. 1,388 players were chosen before him.

- **Woodrow Wilson** was the first president to throw out the first pitch at a World Series game in 1915.

- In 1940, **Bob Feller** threw a no-hitter on opening day.

- Four Hall of Famers once played basketball for the Harlem Globetrotters—**Bob Gibson**, **Ferguson Jenkins**, **Lou Brock**, and **Satchel Paige**.

- In a game between the Cincinnati Reds and Chicago Cubs on June 29, 1913, only one baseball was used for the entire nine-inning game.

- Former teammates **Fernando Valenzuela** and **Dave Stewart** both threw no-hitters on the same day, June 30, 1990. Valenzuela's came for the Dodgers; Stewart's for the Athletics.

- Hillerich & Bradsby cuts about 40,000 trees each season to make Louisville Slugger bats.

- The initials of former Red Sox owners Thomas A. Yawkey and wife Jean R. Yawkey, TAY and JRY, appear in Morse code on the Fenway Park scoreboard.

- In 1948, the Brooklyn Dodgers needed an announcer, and they liked **Ernie Harwell**, who was broadcasting games for the minor league Atlanta Crackers. The Crackers needed a catcher, so the two teams made a deal. The Dodgers traded catcher Cliff Dapper to Atlanta for announcer Harwell.

Sixth INNING

Winning in this game is not just about stars and stats. It is about teams. Great players don't win pennants. Great teams do. To win a championship in baseball requires total team effort, unity, and sacrifice. Great teams succeed because each of the twenty-five or so men that dot the roster throughout the season contributes. Each fills his role. Each man lays down his ego and considers winning above personal glory.

Home runs wow fans. Pitching, defense, clutch hitting, good bullpens, and team play win championships. It is a classic example of the sum of the parts being greater than the whole.

"If you throw a lot of guys together—superstars—a lot

of times it's not going to equate into victories. You have to have

certain pieces that fit together. You need guys who are going

to do the little intangibles that aren't in the box score."

WALT WEISS

"Chemistry is important on every team. I'm not saying that players have to really like one another or get along well off the field, but certainly, when you play on the field, you need good team chemistry. You need guys believing in one another. You need guys picking one another up."

LOU PINIELLA

The New York Yankees of 1998 and '99 are a testimony to the value of teamwork. Two titles in two seasons, yet they had no MVP or Cy Young winners. It was team all the way.

A winning team knows what sacrifice means. One player gives up his own at bat to lay down a bunt and advance a runner. Another takes several good pitches, limiting his hitting options but allowing the runner in front of him every opportunity to steal second base. Yet another hits a seemingly meaningless ground ball to second base, providing for a runner at second to move to third and score one batter later. No one cares how the run scores, who scores the run, or who drives it in; just simply that the run scores.

It's the little things that win games, save seasons, and win titles. Little things don't appear in box scores or contract negotiations. They do show up, however, in those whose passion for the game surpasses their desire for greatness.

"I'm a firm believer you don't treat everyone the same. You don't motivate everyone the same way. Baseball is a people business. We're not dealing with machines . . . but there's no doubt in my mind that we are family."

JOHNNY OATES

"Love is the main ingredient. We bring people here, we make the atmosphere respectful, loving, working hard, projection for the future. We care about their baseball career, their personal life, their domestic life, their spiritual life. When players come into an atmosphere like that, chances are they are going to believe what you teach them."

FELIPE ALOU

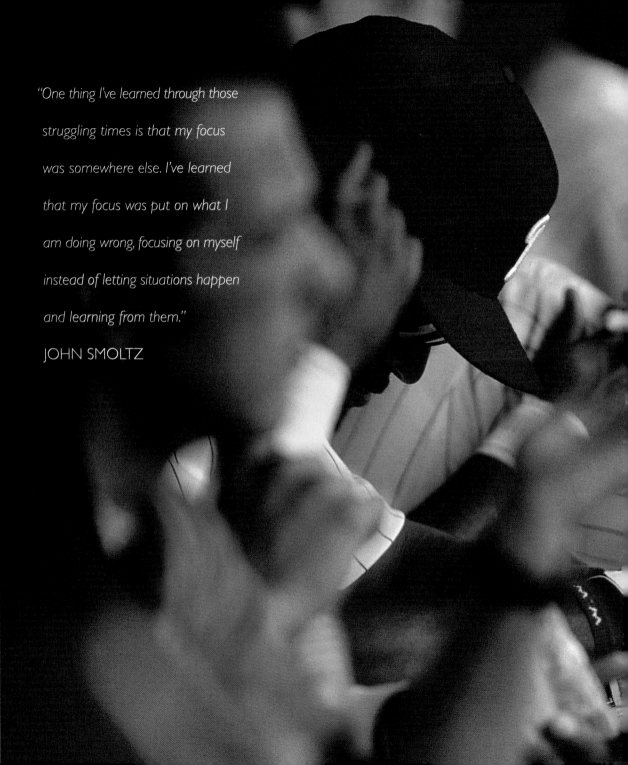

"One thing I've learned through those struggling times is that my focus was somewhere else. I've learned that my focus was put on what I am doing wrong, focusing on myself instead of letting situations happen and learning from them."

JOHN SMOLTZ

"You set a standard as being one of the top pitchers, and you expect that from yourself every year. You come to realize some years are a lot easier to get things done and a lot easier to win ball games, and you just have to hang in there."

ANDY PETTITTE

Seventh INNING

Like life, baseball can be simple, but never easy.

Baseball is a game of adversity. Bad hops, bad breaks, bad calls. Errors, gopher balls, and swings and misses. Slumps, benchings, and demotions to the minors. They are all a part of the game. As in life, very few things are in one's control.

At some point, every pitcher's curveball flattens out; every fastball becomes a bit less fast. To every hitter the ball looks a little smaller than it once did; the extra step on the base paths he once had is nowhere to be found. For some it may only last for a home stand, others a season.

When adversity hits, a player is faced with a choice—to pout or to push on.

"Slump? I ain't in no slump. I just ain't hitting."

YOGI BERRA

"You play through pressure—whether it's from fans, family, or people back home. It was said to me when I was a lot younger that 'excellence can only be measured by yourself.' You can't rely on other people to tell you how good or how bad you are."

TODD WALKER

"Baseball is a game of failure.
No matter what we do, we're not going
to be the perfect ballplayer."

EDDIE TAUBENSEE

"What we went through with my wife was thyroid cancer.
You know, it just takes something like that to bring you
back to focus and get your perspective back. What kind
of character do you have? Is your faith for real? It's been
a great learning experience for both of us."

TIM SALMON

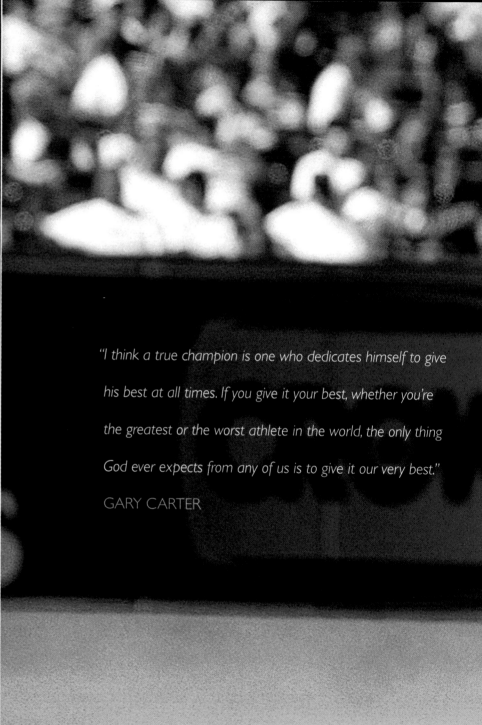

"I think a true champion is one who dedicates himself to give
his best at all times. If you give it your best, whether you're
the greatest or the worst athlete in the world, the only thing
God ever expects from any of us is to give it our very best."

GARY CARTER

In baseball, there is always the next inning, next at bat, the next game. Often the goat in the field just an inning before comes to bat with the bases loaded and the chance to be a hero.

The key is to keep perspective, to not lose passion for the game. Baseball is a game of eternal childhood—where heartthrob and heartbreak go together.

It is through the adversity, in the midst of the crucible—professional and personal—where players discover of what they're made, and why they play the game.

In this place—not in success—champions are forged.

I was twenty-five. I had a wife and a two-year-old daughter, and another one on the way. There was the fear of whether my kids would grow up without a dad. Where is this cancer? Where is it going? What's going to happen? Am I going to live? The answers for me were with Jesus Christ. I sat in the hospital and thought to myself, You know, I can't do this alone."

JERRY DIPOTO

s called the Ross River Fever. It's a mosquito-carried virus during a certain time of the season back in Australia. It's an arthritic virus, and it just knocked me out for a couple f months. I started to wake up and couldn't walk. My wrists, my ankles, my knees, and everything was swollen. I just stayed in bed. I was fortunate enough that after about three months, I was able to make it back onto the field. It put things in perspective."

DAVE NILSSON

"Unfortunately, many of us have to reach a negative point in our lives to really understand that we're not capable of handling this. For me, it was in 1989 when my mother died of cancer. It woke me up to that whole experience, that there's more out there than just us walking the earth."

SCOTT BROSIUS

Baseball was my whole life. For all intents and purposes, I emotionally abandoned my wife and kids and took on the mistress of baseball. My wife and kids were dying in front of me, but I didn't know it, I was so locked into baseball. We got help, I reordered my priorities, and now our marriage is better and our family is closer than ever. I found out that I need them as much as they need me."

JOHNNY OATES

"In 1991 I had a blood clot in my arm…and I went through surgery that lasted almost eleven hours. They took out a vein from my right leg and placed it in my right arm. The doctor said I had a 50 percent chance to come back, but it depended on if I wanted to. That first game back … it was a miracle of God!"

ROBERTO HERNANDEZ

"It really doesn't matter who is standing in the batter's box if you can keep the focus on the mitt and just play catch with your catcher. There are games when I don't even see anybody step in the batter's box."

ANDY PETTITTE

"When you're in 'the zone', it's like a very peaceful, slow-motion, kind of dreamy-like period, because you're just in total control. You're not breathing hard, there's not any anxiety, and you don't feel rushed. You're never caught off guard. You're never too early or too late. Nobody can throw a fastball by you. It's like slow motion."

TIM SALMON

Seventh INNING STRE

Baseball is fickle—one player's fate can seemingly be determined by inches.

The seventh-inning stretch provides a time to pause and look around, take in the atmosphere, assess the situation, and regain perspective.

"There's different reasons why players play the game. I play the game because I grew up with this game. I don't care about the publicity I get. I just like to go out and have fun and do my job."

MIKE JACKSON

TCH

Every player experiences his own seventh-inning stretch. Amidst the daily grind, the unceasing media attention, the money, the headlines, and the roller coaster ride between success and failure, each asks and re-asks the same question. Why do I play the game?

For the player, as with the fan, the answer is simple. When all else is stripped away, one thing remains—the passion for the game.

In his 1948 farewell speech at Yankee Stadium, Babe Ruth called baseball the "only real game." What makes it this are the memories beyond who won, who lost, or who scored. It's the spectacular or botched plays, amazing feats, historic firsts and lasts, streaks, errors, and the endless stream of players.

Not all the memorable players were great, of course. From 5'4" Freddie Patek to Ryne Duren and his Coke-bottle glasses to one-armed Pete Gray, only baseball has given place to men who would find no room in any other sport.

In baseball there are thousands of cherished moments, memorable events, great catches, weird plays, and odd names (consider Nikco Riesgo, Drungo Hazewood, or Van Lingle Mungo).

Baseball is full of delightful players and episodes. In baseball, even mediocre players have had moments of fame. The personalities of the game are remarkably unique—Mark "The Bird" Fidrych, Al Hrabosky, Jimmy Piersall, and Bob Uecker.

What makes baseball irresistible?

Could the answer be no more than the fact that in its own glorious way baseball became the symbol of eternal boyhood? Perhaps. But baseball is also highly complicated, hard-fought, a competitive form of business and sport—which gives it another type of appeal

"A few years ago I realized you have to enjoy the moment, whether you win or lose. This is a game where you have a kid inside you who enjoys the game, and that helps you put the pressure of the game aside."
ROBERTO HERNANDEZ

"I've been catching since I was eight years old, so it comes from the heart."
CHARLES JOHNSON

"My favorite part of the game is when you're out on the field and the game starts and there's no one to bother you. It's like when you played when you were a little kid in Little League; it's so much fun."

EDDIE TAUBENSEE

"It's a bunch of old guys out here playing a kid's game— it's always been a lot of fun."

J. D. DREW

Eighth INNING

The game endures because it reflects the American character. The game, like our own life experience, is filled with comebacks.

In the landscape of baseball, any player can become a Bobby Thomson, any team the "Miracle Mets."

Pennant chases are all about being down but not out.

"Day in and day out you've got to come to the ballpark and still be excited about being here. You have to stay positive and say, 'This is the day I'm going to get three hits!'"

TODD WALKER

"You can't have a miracle every day— except you can when you get great pitching."

CASEY STENGEL

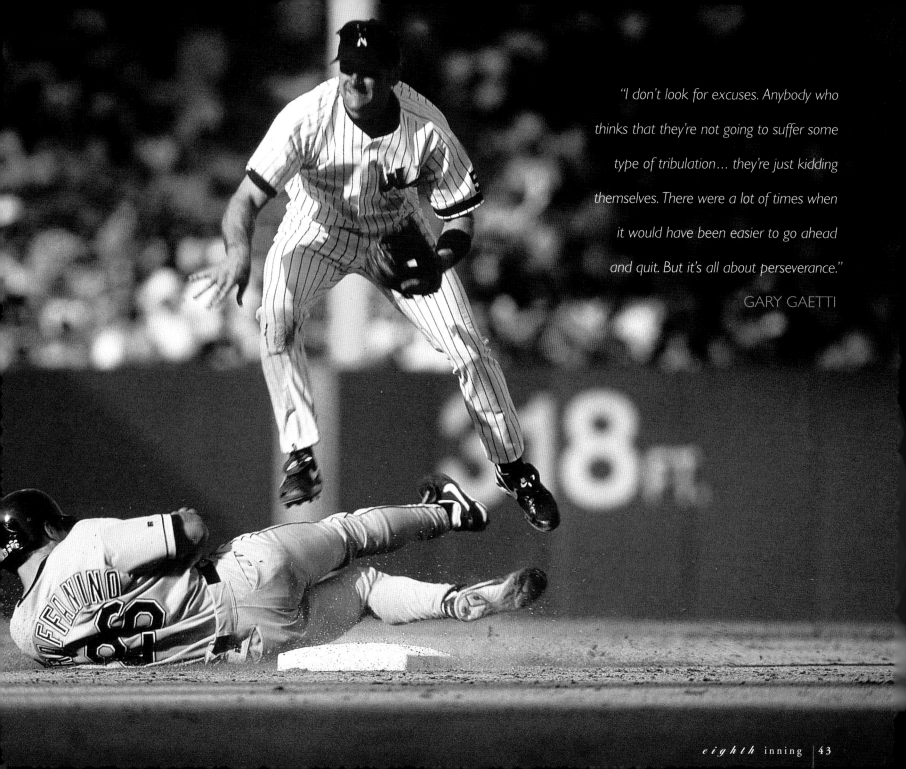

"I don't look for excuses. Anybody who thinks that they're not going to suffer some type of tribulation… they're just kidding themselves. There were a lot of times when it would have been easier to go ahead and quit. But it's all about perseverance."

GARY GAETTI

Getting the clutch hit late in the game. Wanting the ball hit to you at the most crucial moment. Making a great catch, a great throw. Ringing up an inning-ending strikeout with the bases loaded. Breaking up a double play. Laying it all on the line. Anyone can swing the momentum of the game, change the complexion.

Moments in the sun turn into days in the spotlight.

While the game is complex, it seemingly always comes down to the simple challenge of pitcher versus hitter, with outcomes as unpredictable as the men who orchestrate them. So endless are the possibilities, often we gain the impression that the game will adjust itself to meet the apex of every important game or series.

And sometimes it does.

As Yogi Berra told us about this game, "It ain't over 'til it's over."

"You feel like it's the end of the world if you lose

or if you're in a bad slump. Then, a week later, everything

changes and the sun comes up again."

PAUL O'NEILL

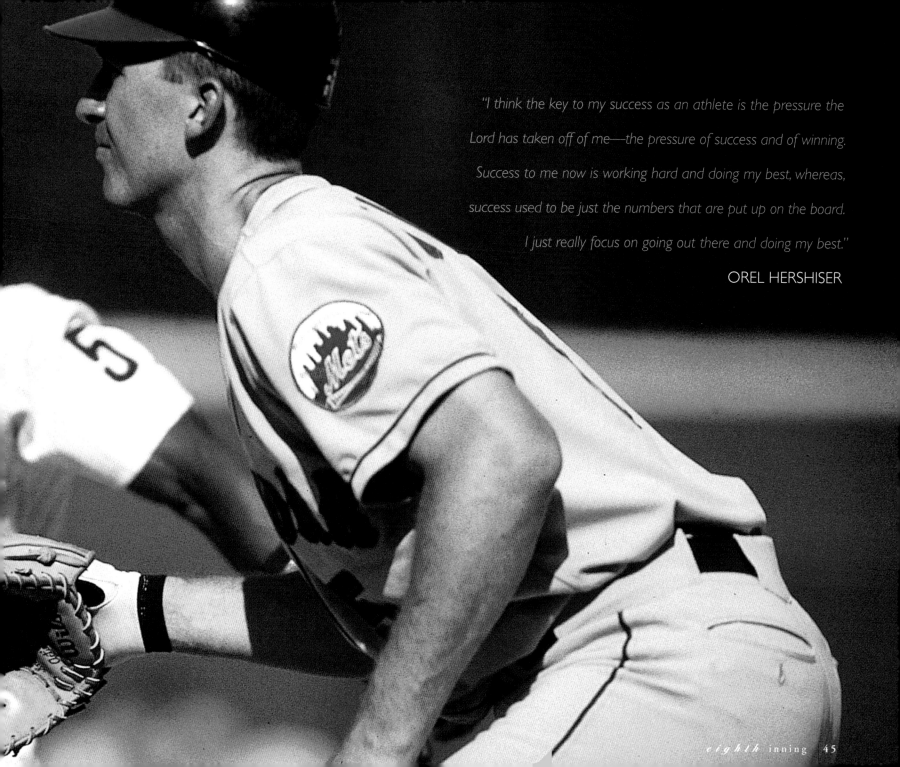

"I think the key to my success as an athlete is the pressure the
Lord has taken off of me—the pressure of success and of winning.
Success to me now is working hard and doing my best, whereas,
success used to be just the numbers that are put up on the board.
I just really focus on going out there and doing my best."

OREL HERSHISER

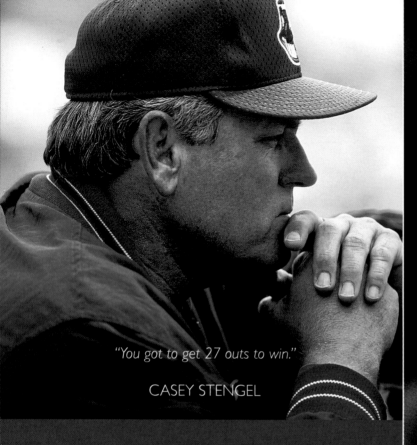

"You got to get 27 outs to win."

CASEY STENGEL

"When you play, you play to win. A lot of people don't understand that. A lot of people just play to have fun. I've always played to win. I think that if you don't play to win, there's no reason to keep score."

PAUL O'NEILL

"The best part of the game is just standing on the mound in the ninth inning—just the competition of it all. The biggest thrill is when you can get on that mound in the ninth inning and have a chance to save a ball game and get a victory for your ball club."

RICK AGUILERA

Ninth INNING

Nothing is more deflating than to wind up just short at the end. The end of the game, the end of the season, the end of life.

In baseball, everything is focused toward finishing on top.

"You can be a hero one day and a bum the
next. If you hit a home run tonight, you're a
hero. If you strike out with the bases loaded
the next night, you're a bum. And the fans
are very fickle. We know life itself is fickle.
But we do know that Jesus is always the
same, yesterday, today, and tomorrow.
He doesn't care how many hits you got.
He gives you the gift of salvation no
matter what your record is."

ERNIE HARWELL

"I used to be a young man who blew where the wind blew. Now there's a purpose. There's an eternal purpose, and not just in what I do, but in how I know I'm being watched. How does Jesus Christ view me? Well, I was precious enough to be won over by His blood, and that's how much He loves and cares for me. I try and keep that perspective in terms of looking at everything else."

JOHN WETTELAND

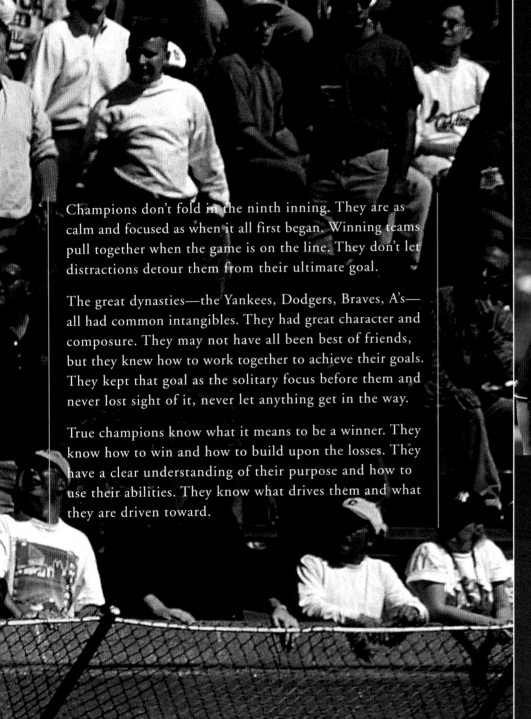

Champions don't fold in the ninth inning. They are as calm and focused as when it all first began. Winning teams pull together when the game is on the line. They don't let distractions detour them from their ultimate goal.

The great dynasties—the Yankees, Dodgers, Braves, A's—all had common intangibles. They had great character and composure. They may not have all been best of friends, but they knew how to work together to achieve their goals. They kept that goal as the solitary focus before them and never lost sight of it, never let anything get in the way.

True champions know what it means to be a winner. They know how to win and how to build upon the losses. They have a clear understanding of their purpose and how to use their abilities. They know what drives them and what they are driven toward.

"A relief pitcher comes in the last inning, and all the emotion and everyone are focused on that last inning. They may forget about the first eight innings, but if you make a mistake in the ninth, they remember that you lost the game."

ROBERTO HERNANDEZ

"I realize that the Lord is the right way. I play to glorify Him, and it takes the pressure off, because I realize that it's in His hands. It's so easy to get off track, but by really knowing Jesus, He's the way. He's your focus and keeps you on the right path."

ALEX RODRIGUEZ

"Jesus is the way, the truth, and the life, and nobody goes to the Father except through Him. Our time here is a vapor, and eternity is a long, long time. So, it was a no-brainer that I wanted to know Christ so I could spend eternity with Him in heaven."

ANTHONY TELFORD

BOTTOM OF THE *Ninth*

Collectively, the crowd stands to its feet. Tension is almost given texture. It is the ultimate challenge—the "closer" versus the "slugger." It is my team against yours. Good versus evil. It is the defining moment; the moment of truth. The outcome of the entirety of the struggle will be determined here. And then it will end.

"I realize that this game is not going to last forever . . . the thing we all have to realize is that sooner or later, we're all going to die. And certainly, these things, they may be remembered, but in the end, the perspective we have is we have a choice to make. We're either going to heaven or hell, and it's our choice. The thing I want to do is be able to live forever."

JAY BELL

The closer's job is to get the "save"; to secure victory.

So it is in life. There is a save opportunity. Then the game is over.

Here, the stakes are infinitely higher. Victory and loss are eternal. Each save goes into a record book that will never fade.

In the heart of a champion, no victory is greater.

For these men, their passion for the game is exceeded only by a passion for the One who gained the ultimate save for them.

Extra INNINGS

"God is powerful. He is a friend who never fails. God is peace, happiness, and in the moments of sadness and pain, Jesus Christ never fails you."

JUAN GONZALEZ

What we remember about baseball after the game or season is over is its unforgettable moments—the impossible catch, the towering home run, the stolen base, the big strikeout. Etched in our minds are the images of the best of the best.

No player exemplified the "best" more than Mickey Charles Mantle. A hero to two generations, he was—for a time—bigger than the game itself. For many fans today, he remains the epitome of baseball.

A small-town country kid from Commerce, Oklahoma, Mantle was raised on a farm with the dream of becoming a big leaguer. He had a simple, boyish naïveté about him that instantly endeared him to a baseball public that was screaming for a new hero. Young, blond, shy, and strong, he was a legend in the making.

A switch-hitter, he had frightening power from either side of the plate. He hit the ball farther than most had ever seen. Genuinely fearing him, pitchers often walked Mickey. But having him on the base paths was just as harmful. He possessed blinding speed, once circling the bases faster than any human before him. In the field, he had an unusually strong arm, cat-quick reactions, and an uncanny knack for reading nearly any ball hit his way. He was quickly labeled by fans and experts alike as the "greatest player who ever lived."

Through world championships, pennant races, the triple crown, and home run titles, the bigger the game, the more Mickey seemed to rise to the occasion. The World Series record book seems to be an abridged Mantle autobiography.

536 career home runs and a bevy of records—all lessened by a succession of catastrophic leg injuries. Only God knows what many have pondered—"What might have been?"

He was baseball's golden boy; the real "Natural"; an idol.

"I think God has given me the ability to play baseball.

It's my responsibility to work hard and do the best job I can.

But as far as results, and what's going to happen in the future,

it's really given me peace to know that God has

a plan for me. He's in control."

JOHN OLERUD

Yet on the inside, the road of adversity and a series of bad choices were insidiously taking their toll on this "hero." We were later to find out what many surmised all along. This man among men was still just a kid at heart. The folly of youth began to deteriorate his body and depress the soul.

In the blink of an eye, the valiant hero was nearly gone. Wracked with cancer, he was down to his last at bat. Yet it was the Mick's opportunity for a save. An old teammate who helped Mantle capture seven American League pennants and three World Series came through with one last assist.

Former Yankee second baseman Bobby Richardson walked into Mickey's hospital room as the bottom of the ninth began.

"His mind was crystal clear. He said, 'Bobby, it's so good to see ya.' And I said, 'Mickey, I love ya, and I just want you to spend eternity with me.' We had talked about the Lord many times before, and he said, 'That's what I wanted to tell ya. I just wanted to let you know that I've accepted Christ and I'm a Christian.'

"I said, 'Mickey, that's wonderful! Let's just go over it to make sure.' And I just went over God's plan of salvation in a simple way that God loved us and had a plan and a purpose for our lives and sent the Lord Jesus Christ to shed His precious blood. God promised in His Word that if he would repent of his sin and receive the Lord Jesus, he might not only have everlasting life but the joy of letting Him live His life in him. Mickey said, 'That's just what I've done.'

"My wife, Betsy, knelt down by him and held his hand. Then she asked him the question, 'Mickey, if God were here today, and He would ask you the question, 'Why should I let you into my heaven?' what would you say?'

"His first response was, 'We're talking about God?' And she said, 'That's right, Mickey, we are.' Then he quoted John 3:16: 'For God so loved the world that He gave His only begotten son that whosoever believeth in Him should not perish but have everlasting life.'

"I don't know whether it was in the quietness of the moment with the Holy Spirit that he made a decision, or whether there were others that prompted him, but I do know that he made a decision for Christ, and that he had a peace there at the end.

"I was just absolutely thrilled! Not because it was Mickey Mantle, but because it was a close friend, and one who would spend eternity with Christ."

Buoyed by his newfound faith, the hero who had slipped from his pedestal decided to take one last cut. It was the biggest hit of his life.

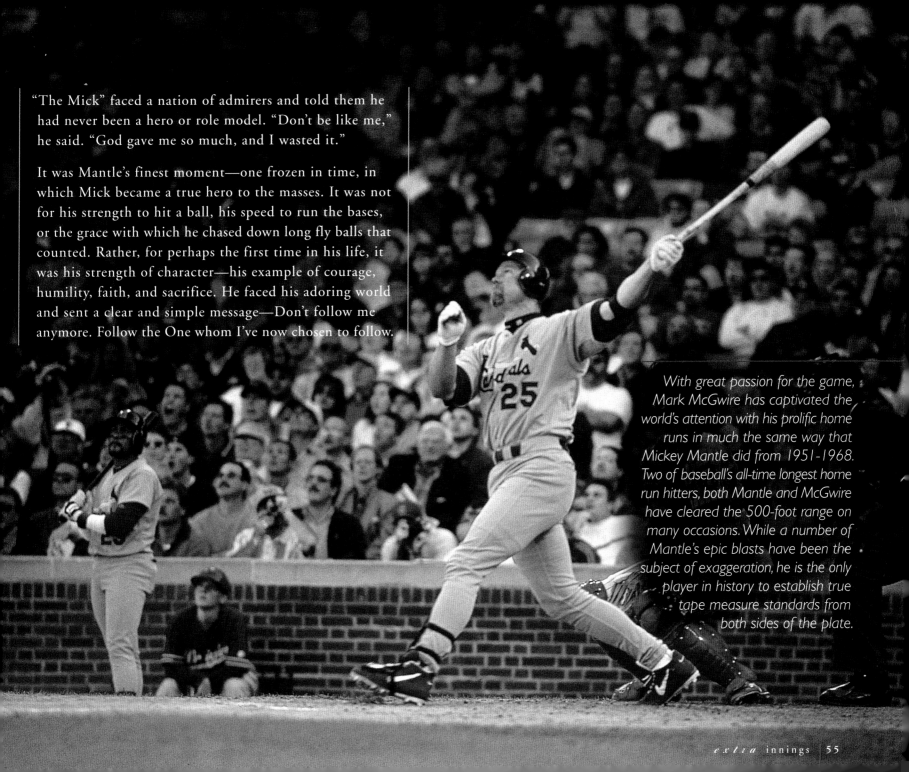

"The Mick" faced a nation of admirers and told them he had never been a hero or role model. "Don't be like me," he said. "God gave me so much, and I wasted it."

It was Mantle's finest moment—one frozen in time, in which Mick became a true hero to the masses. It was not for his strength to hit a ball, his speed to run the bases, or the grace with which he chased down long fly balls that counted. Rather, for perhaps the first time in his life, it was his strength of character—his example of courage, humility, faith, and sacrifice. He faced his adoring world and sent a clear and simple message—Don't follow me anymore. Follow the One whom I've now chosen to follow.

With great passion for the game, Mark McGwire has captivated the world's attention with his prolific home runs in much the same way that Mickey Mantle did from 1951-1968. Two of baseball's all-time longest home run hitters, both Mantle and McGwire have cleared the 500-foot range on many occasions. While a number of Mantle's epic blasts have been the subject of exaggeration, he is the only player in history to establish true tape measure standards from both sides of the plate.

Heart of a Champion is a registered trademark under which virtuous sports products and programs are created and distributed. Materials include award-winning videos, television and radio programs, films, books, and internet activities. To learn more about Heart of a Champion resources, products, or programs, call 1-800-981-9298 or visit the web site at www.heartofachampion.com.

The Heart of a Champion Foundation is an independent national non-profit organization utilizing the platform of sports to build and reinforce character and ethics in young people. Blending the message and the messenger, the Heart of a Champion Foundation's winning formula teaches and models character education at the grassroots level, to mold better citizens and develop the heart of a champion in youth. For more information, visit the web site at www.heartofachampion.org. or call (972) 497-8538.

Additional copies of this book and other titles from Honor Books are available from your local bookstore.

If you have enjoyed this book or it has impacted your life, we would like you to hear from you. Please contact us at:

Honor Books
Department E
P.O. Box 55388
Tulsa, Oklahoma 74155

or by e-mail at: info@honorbooks.com

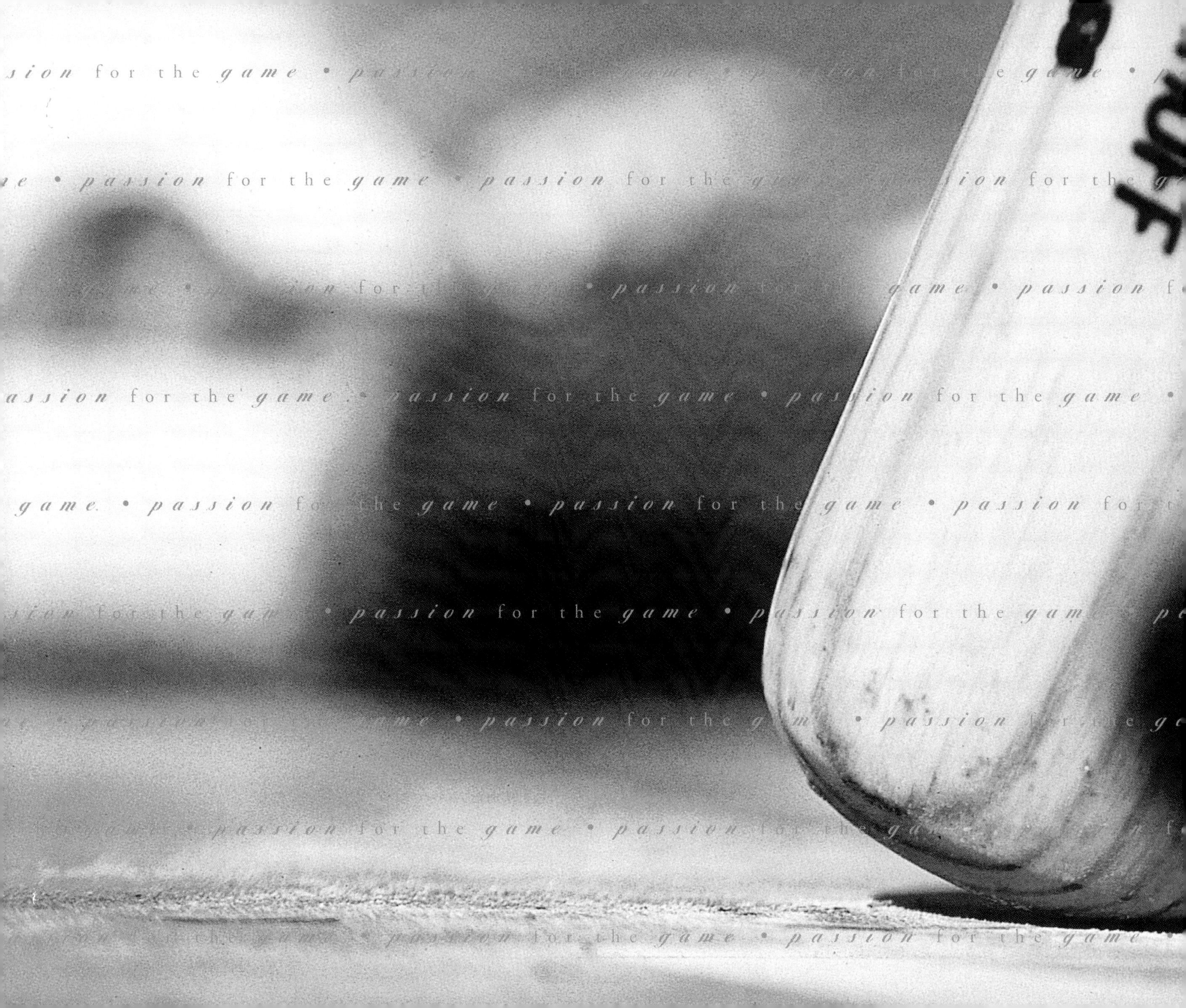
passion for the game